KU-312-653

Contents

Some words are printed in bold, **like this**. You can find out what they mean in the glossary. You can also look in the box at the bottom of the page where the word first appears.

WHAT ARE MUMMIES?

When a dead body is buried, it decays over time. The body breaks down and becomes part of the soil. Only the bones are left.

How mummies are made

A mummy is a dead body that has not decayed. Mummies have skin. They can even have hair or fingernails.

Some mummies are made by humans. Other dead bodies have become mummies because they were left in places, like **bogs**, where they did not decay.

STRANGE BUT TRUE!

Some mummies have been found still wearing clothes.

bog	soft, muddy ground
decay	rot slowly

MUMMIES

MARC TYLER NOBLEMAN

ALIS
1773504

www.raintreepublishers.co.uk
Visit our website to find out more information about **Raintree** books.

To order:
📞 Phone 44 (0) 1865 888112
📄 Send a fax to 44 (0) 1865 314091
💻 Visit the Raintree bookshop at **www.raintreepublishers.co.uk** to browse our catalogue and order online.

First published in Great Britain by
Raintree, Halley Court, Jordan Hill,
Oxford OX2 8EJ, part of Harcourt
Education. Raintree is a registered
trademark of Harcourt Education Ltd.

© Harcourt Education Ltd 2007
First published in paperback in 2007.
The moral right of the proprietor has been asserted.

All rights reserved. No part of this publication
may be reproduced, stored in a retrieval system, or
transmitted in any form or by any means, electronic,
mechanical, photocopying, recording, or otherwise,
without either the prior written permission of the
publishers or a licence permitting restricted copying
in the United Kingdom issued by the Copyright
Licensing Agency Ltd, 90 Tottenham Court Road,
London W1T 4LP (www.cla.co.uk).

Editorial: Louise Galpine, Rosie Gordon,
Dave Harris, and Stig Vatland
Design: Victoria Bevan and Bigtop
Picture Research: Hannah Taylor and Sally Claxton
Production: Camilla Crask
Originated by Chroma Graphics Pte. Ltd
Printed and bound in China by WKT

10 digit ISBN 1 406 20344 0 (hardback)
13 digit ISBN 978 1 4062 0344 8
11 10 09 08 07
10 9 8 7 6 5 4 3 2 1

10 digit ISBN 1 406 20365 3 (paperback)
13 digit ISBN 978 1 4062 0365 3
12 11 10 09 08
10 9 8 7 6 5 4 3 2 1

J393·3
1773504

British Library Cataloguing in Publication Data
Nobleman, Marc Tyler
Mummies. – (Atomic)
393.3
A full catalogue record for this book is available
from the British Library.

Acknowledgements
The publishers would like to thank the following
for permission to reproduce photographs: p. **6**,
Corbis Royalty Free; pp. **20 & 21**, Corbis Sygma;
p. **17**, Corbis Sygma/Jeffery Newbury; p. **26**, Corbis/
Bettmann; p. **22**, Corbis/Chris Lisle; p. **25**, Corbis/
Hulton Deutsch Collection; p. **18**, Corbis/Reuters;
pp. **28 & 29**, Corbis/Reuters/Handout/Supreme
Council for Antiquities; p. **10**, Corbis/Roger Wood;
p. **24**, Getty Images/Hulton Archive; pp. **12 & 13**,
Getty Images/Time Life Pictures; p. **5**, Science Photo
Library/National Museum of Denmark/Munoz-
Yague; p. **14** b, p. **14** t, The Art Archive/Musee du
Louvre, Paris/Dagli Orti. Cover: Getty Images/Taxi.

The publishers would like to thank Diana Bentley,
Nancy Harris, and Dee Reid for their assistance in
the preparation of this book.

Every effort has been made to contact copyright
holders of any material reproduced in this book.
Any omissions will be rectified in subsequent
printings if notice is given to the publishers.

Disclaimer
All the Internet addresses (URLs) given in this book
were valid at the time of going to press. However,
due to the dynamic nature of the Internet, some
addresses may have changed, or sites may have
changed or ceased to exist since publication. While
the author and publishers regret any inconvenience
this may cause readers, no responsibility for any
such changes can be accepted by either the author
or the publishers.

This mummy was found in a bog in Denmark in 1879.

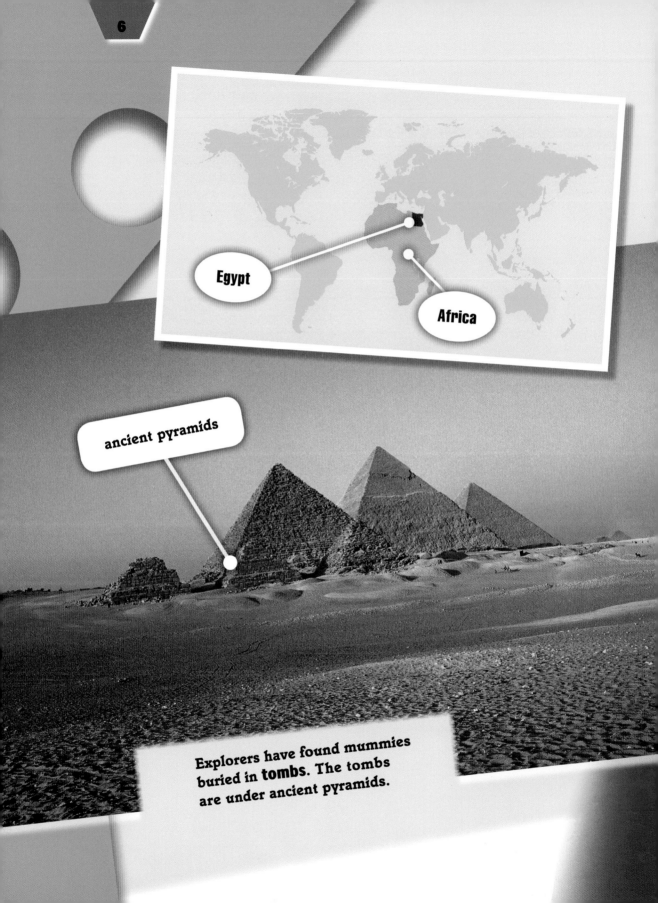

Egypt

Africa

ancient pyramids

Explorers have found mummies buried in **tombs**. The tombs are under ancient pyramids.

ANCIENT EGYPT

Egypt is a country in northern Africa (see map). Ancient Egyptians buried mummies in tombs. They built huge **pyramids** over the tombs.

The afterlife

Many people believe in an **afterlife**. This is where people go when they die. Ancient Egyptians believed that you needed your body in the afterlife, so they prepared bodies for the afterlife with special treatments. These treatments turned the bodies into mummies.

WHAT DO YOU THINK?

Would you like your body to be made into a mummy?

afterlife	life after death
pyramid	building with four sides shaped like triangles
tomb	place where a person is buried

MAKING MUMMIES

In ancient Egypt, it took 70 days to make a mummy.

A delicate job

Priests used a hook to remove the brain. They pulled it out through the mummy's nose! They also cut open the body and removed the lungs and other **organs**, but left the heart.

Priests dried the body with salt. Then, they stuffed it with sawdust or leaves. Finally, they oiled the body and wrapped it in linen (cloth).

STRANGE BUT TRUE!

The Egyptians left only the heart in the body. They believed it was the organ of intelligence.

organ	body part that has a special task
priest	person who performs religious ceremonies

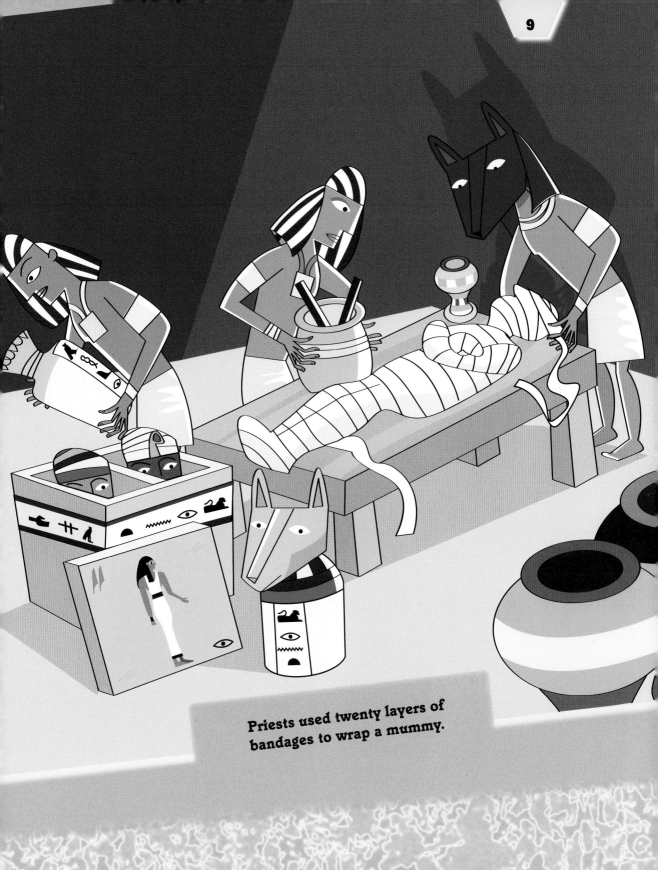

Priests used twenty layers of bandages to wrap a mummy.

This is the death mask of King Tutankhamen. It was found in his tomb.

Boy to King to Mummy

Tutankhamen became king of Egypt 3,000 years ago. He was only a young boy. He died when he was nineteen years old. After he died, he was made into a mummy.

Finding Tut

In 1922, explorer Howard Carter discovered a **tomb** in Egypt. Inside he found Tutankhamen's mummy.

Some people were amazed. Others were afraid. Ancient Egyptians had warned that bad things would happen to anyone who disturbed the dead. However, Carter was not afraid. He wanted to learn more about ancient Egypt from "King Tut".

WHAT DO YOU THINK?

Should Carter have disturbed the tomb of King Tut?

A Mummy Curse?

After Howard Carter found Tutankhamen's tomb, scary things started to happen. A cobra ate Carter's pet canary. Lord Carnarvon, who paid for Carter's trip to Egypt, suddenly died.

Strange events

Some people say that ten more people connected to opening Tut's **tomb** died. A legend says that the lights went out in Cairo, Egypt, at the moment Lord Carnarvon died. However, Carter lived for seventeen more years.

WHAT DO YOU THINK?

Was there a curse on King Tut's tomb?

People thought that Carter's crew was cursed after opening the tomb.

curse   bad luck spell

People have mummified cats, monkeys, and even crocodiles.

ANIMAL MUMMIES

It was not only people that the ancient Egyptians mummified. They also mummified animals.

Why did Egyptians mummify animals?

Sometimes they mummified animals they thought were **sacred**, such as bulls. Other times they mummified animals as gifts for their gods. They also mummified animals as food for human mummies in the **afterlife**.

STRANGE BUT TRUE!

Some types of fish that the Egyptians mummified are now **extinct**.

extinct   no longer existing

sacred   holy

MUMMIES IN CHINA

In the 1900s, explorers found mummies in the deserts of China (see map). Dry weather **preserved** these Chinese mummies. But scientists say that the mummies were not Chinese people.

Who were these mummies?

Some people think that these mummies were foreign traders. The traders may have travelled to China thousands of years ago. These mummies help scientists understand how far early people might have travelled.

China

preserve	stop something from rotting

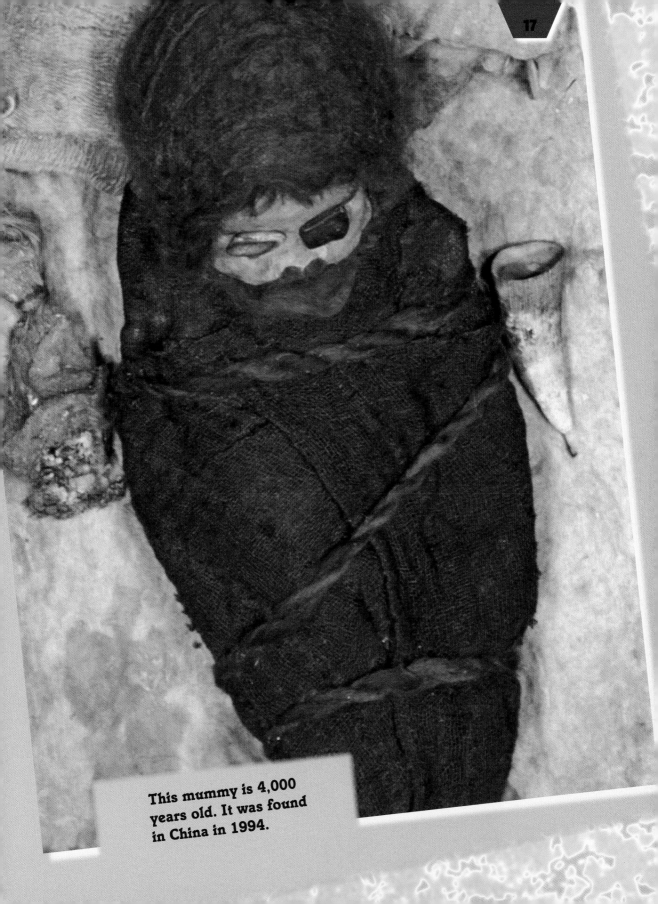

This mummy is 4,000 years old. It was found in China in 1994.

South America

Peru

Chile

Some Incan children
were mummified.

MUMMIES IN SOUTH AMERICA

The oldest known mummies are from South America. They were found in Chile (see map). The Chinchoros tribe made mummies there 7,000 years ago.

Are all mummies the same?

The Chinchoros did not make mummies in the same way as the ancient Egyptians. They cut up the body. Then they added chemicals to **preserve** the **organs**. They put the body back together with straw and sticks. Then they covered it with mud.

The Incan people of Peru also made mummies. These were not as ancient as the Chinchoros mummies. The Incan mummies were made about 1,000 years ago.

STRANGE BUT TRUE!

The Incan mummies were found on high mountains. It is hard for people to breathe at this height. People are not sure how the mummies got there.

ICE MUMMIES

Sometimes mummies are not made by people. They are made by nature. In 1991, hikers found a man's body frozen on a mountaintop. It was 5,000 years old. This mummy became known as the Iceman.

Mummy on Mount Everest

In 1924, an adventurer named George Mallory tried to climb Mount Everest. Everest is the world's tallest mountain. Mallory never came back. Then, in 1999, mountain climbers found Mallory's body. The cold air had **preserved** it.

WHAT DO YOU THINK?

Do you think there might be other ice mummies to be discovered?

This is the Iceman. He was found on this mountainside with a grass cape and a bow and arrow.

The bog mummy's skin has become very dark over the centuries.

BOG MUMMIES

A bog is an area of wet ground. There is little or no air below the surface of a bog. That means bodies stuck in bogs may mummify rather than decay.

Where are bog mummies found?

Bog mummies have been found in northern Europe. Bog mummies are often well **preserved**. Scientists can find out how they died. But why are they in the bog?

STRANGE BUT TRUE!

A bog mummy could be someone who was murdered. Their body could have been thrown into a bog. Could the murderer guess that the body would be discovered 2,000 years later?

MODERN MUMMIES

Some people want to be mummified when they die. Jeremy Bentham wanted his body to be **preserved.** After he died in 1832, his body was mummified. His head was replaced with a wax copy.

Preserving loved ones

Eva Perón was the wife of a president of Argentina in South America. She died in 1952 and her body was mummified.

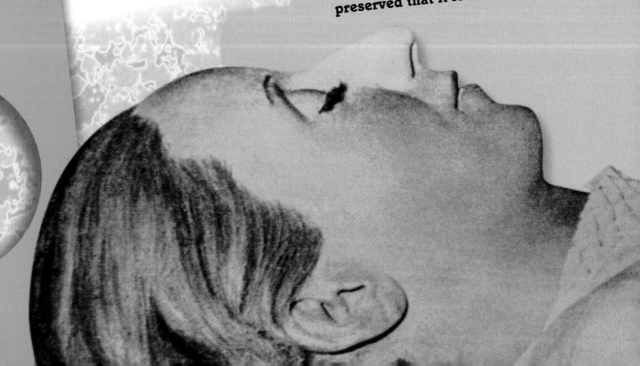

Perón's body was so well preserved that it looked alive.

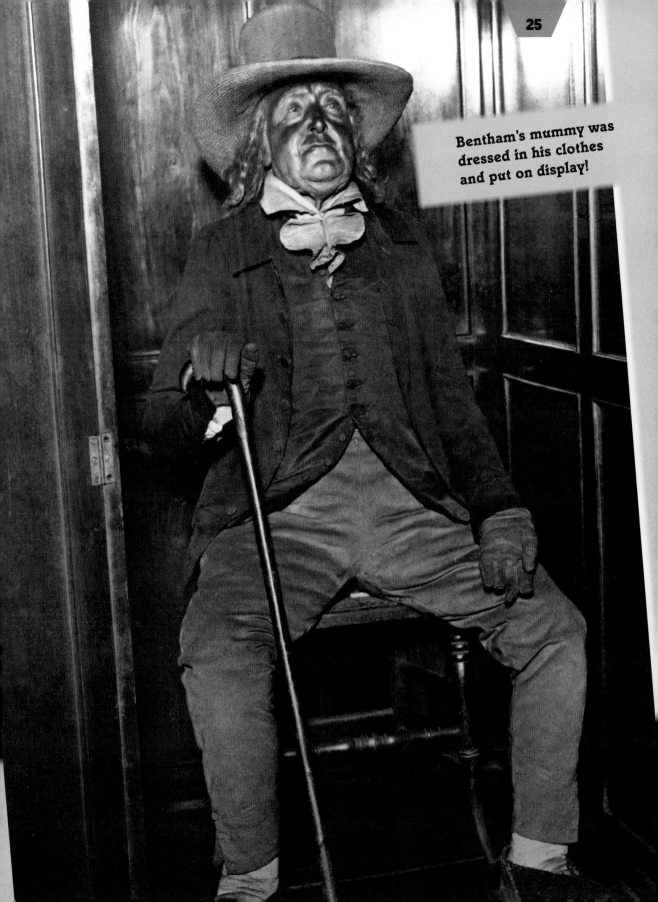

Bentham's mummy was dressed in his clothes and put on display!

In the 1932 film, Im-Ho-Tep tries to find the woman he loved – and scares people along the way.

MUMMIES IN FILMS

In 1932, a film called *The Mummy* was made. This horror film is about Im-Ho-Tep, an ancient Egyptian prince. He was a criminal and to punish him he was buried alive. Thousands of years later, the mummy of Im-Ho-Tep comes to life.

Modern mummies

Since *The Mummy*, mummies have often been monsters in cartoons and films. Usually the mummies in films come back to life.

WHAT DO YOU THINK?

Why are there so many stories about mummies coming back to life?

MUMMIES ARE TEACHERS

Mummies can tell us a lot about the past.

Inside mummies

By studying mummies, we can know about people who lived thousands of years ago. We know that they looked like we do. We also know how they dressed.

However, some people believe it is best not to disturb a mummy. They think we should respect a mummy and leave it alone.

What do you think?

STRANGE BUT TRUE!

Some scientists remove food pieces from a mummy's stomach. We can learn what a mummy's last meal was!

X-ray   machine that allows us to see inside something

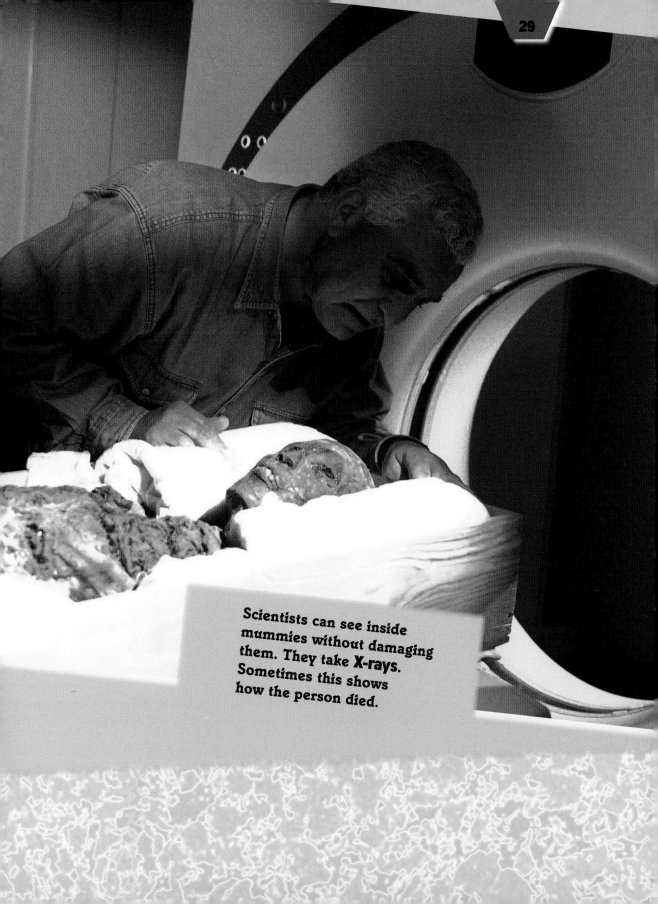

Scientists can see inside mummies without damaging them. They take **X-rays**. Sometimes this shows how the person died.

Glossary

afterlife life after death

bog soft, muddy ground

curse bad luck spell

decay rot slowly

extinct no longer existing

organ body part that has a special task

preserve stop something from rotting

priest person who performs religious ceremonies

pyramid building with four sides shaped like triangles

sacred holy

tomb place where a person is buried

X-ray machine that allows us to see inside something

Want to Know More?

Books

* *Eyewitness Guides: Mummy*, James Putnam (Dorling Kindersley, 2003)

* *My Best Book of Mummies*, Philip Steele (Kingfisher Books Ltd, 2000)

* *You Wouldn't Want to Be an Egyptian Mummy*, David Stewart (Franklin Watts, 2000)

Websites

* www.ancientegypt.co.uk
Click on "mummification" to find lots of Egyptian mummy facts.

* www.mummytombs.com
This site has a quiz and information about mummies from all over the world.

* www.si.umich.edu/CHICO/mummy
Learn more about how the Egyptians made mummies.

If you liked this Atomic book, why don't you try these...?

Index

Notes for adults

Use the following questions to guide children towards identifying features of discussion text:

Can you find examples of present tense language on page 4?
Can you give an example of a statement of the issue from page 7?
Can you find examples of different opinions on page 11?
Can you find an example of a logical connective on page 12?
Can you give an example of summary on page 28?